Contents

Honda – living the dream

Honda was formed in Japan in the 1940s by Mr Soichiro Honda. Today, it makes more motorbikes per year than any other company. Honda began by making only motorbikes, but now also makes cars, speedboats, trucks and many other power products.

Innovation

A major part of Honda's success has come from developing new ideas and working closely with customers. Honda has produced some motorbike innovations, including the first bike with an automatic gearbox, called the Hondamatic. In 2006, the company announced the first motorbike airbag (see page 21).

(see page 21)

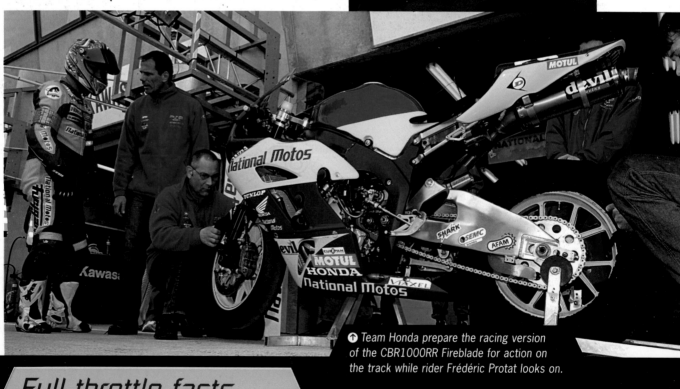

↑ Team Honda prepare the racing version of the CBR1000RR Fireblade for action on the track while rider Frédéric Protat looks on.

Full throttle facts

Company name: Honda Motor Company Ltd
Year of founding: 1948
First bike model: Dream D

Employees: 179,060
Headquarters: Tokyo, Japan
President: Mr Takenoku Ito

RED-HOT BIKES
HONDA

Clive Gifford

FRANKLIN WATTS

This edition 2012

First published in 2007 by
Franklin Watts
338 Euston Road
London NW1 3BH

Franklin Watts Australia
Level 17/207 Kent Street
Sydney NSW 2000

Series editor: Adrian Cole
Series design: Big Blu
Art director: Jonathan Hair

A CIP catalogue record for this book is available from the British Library.

ISBN: 978 1 4451 0736 3

Dewey Classification: 629.227'5

Acknowledgements:
The Publisher would like to thank Honda UK
All images © Honda Motor Europe Limited
Every attempt has been made to clear copyright. Should there be any
inadvertent omission please apply to the publisher for rectification.

Printed in China

Franklin Watts is a division of Hachette Children's Books,
an Hachette UK company.
www.hachette.co.uk

Into racing

Soichiro Honda's childhood dream was to be motorbike world champion, riding one of his own machines. Honda motorbikes have been involved in motor racing since the 1950s. They have won World Superbike and World GP500 championships, as well as off-road competitions such as the Baja 1000. Honda motorbikes have won the Baja 1000 a record 13 times and notched up an incredible 600 GP wins.

➲ The CBR1000RR Fireblade is a powerful road bike that has tasted success in circuit racing, including TT Superbike and Le Mans 24-hour wins.

The Honda Zoomer was first released in the UK in 2005.

Current models

Today, Honda produces a wide range of motorbikes and motor scooters. These vary in size and speed from the small but nippy Zoomer scooter up to the large and powerful Honda Gold Wing GL1800. In this book you will get up close to six of Honda's most popular and exciting machines.

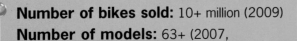

Number of bikes sold: 10+ million (2009)
Number of models: 63+ (2007, including scooters)

Best-selling model: CRF50F (2011)
Number of manufacturing plants: 120 (including cars and other vehicles)

Honda CB600F Hornet

Naked bikes are a special class of motorbike. They are stripped of any fairing to give them a lean, mean street look. Naked bikes are designed for high performance and top speed. The Honda CB600F is also called the Hornet. It was first introduced in 1998. The Hornet was one of the first naked bikes. It is a fast, reliable machine that has helped to make naked bikes popular with riders, especially in Europe.

⬆ A test driver takes a Hornet into a tight turn. Nothing about the Hornet is slow or sluggish and that includes its sharp and simple styling.

Full throttle facts

Top speed: 225 kph +
Length: 2,090 mm

Ground clearance: 135 mm
Fuel capacity: 19 litres

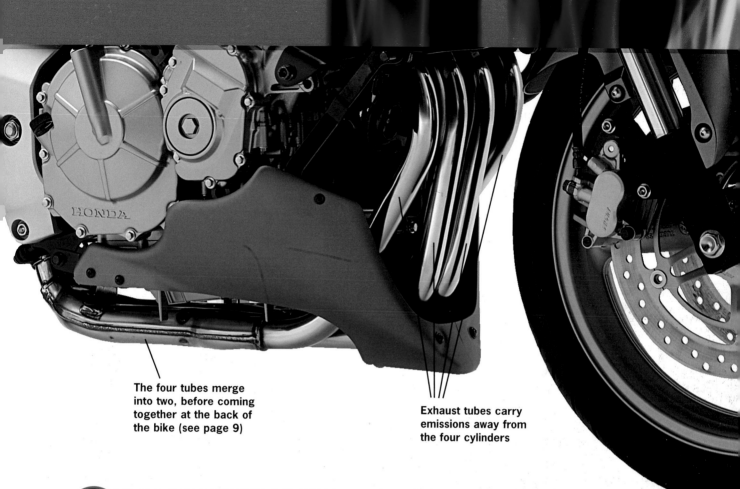

The four tubes merge into two, before coming together at the back of the bike (see page 9)

Exhaust tubes carry emissions away from the four cylinders

HOT SPOT

Exhausts

The Hornet has a 4-cylinder 600 cc engine. The waste gases, called exhaust emissions, are carried out of each cylinder by an exhaust tube which merges first into two and finally one rear exhaust outlet on the righthand side of the bike. This 4 into 2 into 1 exhaust system produces a throaty sound as the bike accelerates.

Tech talk

Accelerates – increases speed.

Fairing – a shell, usually made of plastic or fibreglass, fitted over the frame of some motorbikes to shield the rider and chassis from the wind.

Fuel capacity – the maximum amount of fuel that can be held by the petrol tank.

Kerb weight – the total weight of a motorbike with standard equipment and liquids including oil, coolant and a full tank of fuel but not with a rider.

Kerb weight: 198 kg
Seat height: 800 mm

Engine capacity: 600 cc
Gearbox: 6-speed

Model development

The first major update of the Hornet came with the new model in 2000. Its front wheel was 25 mm larger in diameter, its tail was shorter and it featured better brakes. The next major update occurred in 2003 when the engine was retuned for more speed. The suspension was changed for a more stable ride. The 2003 model also featured: a 17-litre fuel tank; a twin-bulb headlight; squared-up side mirrors instead of round ones and re-designed indicator lamps. In 2007 the Hornet featured an enlarged fuel tank and a re-designed instrument panel. It included a large tachometer dial and an electronic LCD display (see opposite page).

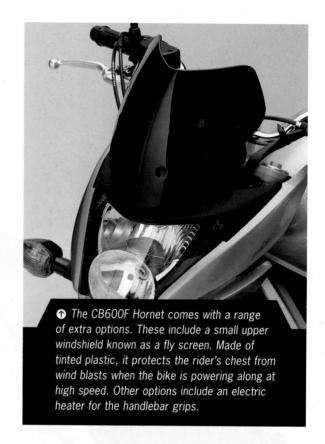

⬆ The CB600F Hornet comes with a range of extra options. These include a small upper windshield known as a fly screen. Made of tinted plastic, it protects the rider's chest from wind blasts when the bike is powering along at high speed. Other options include an electric heater for the handlebar grips.

Honda CB600F

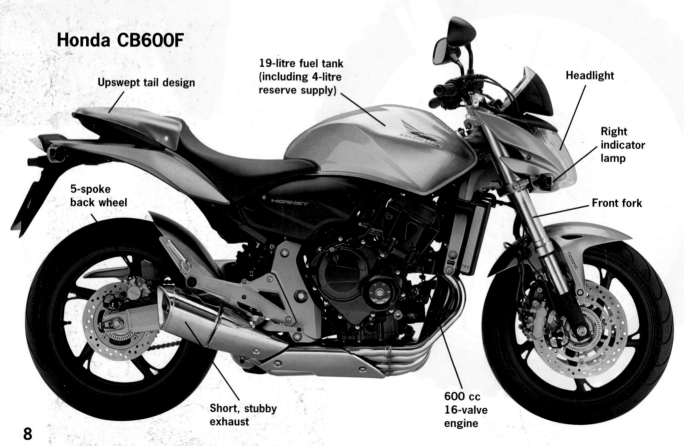

Upswept tail design

19-litre fuel tank (including 4-litre reserve supply)

Headlight

Right indicator lamp

5-spoke back wheel

Front fork

Short, stubby exhaust

600 cc 16-valve engine

HISS

HISS stands for Honda Ignition Security System. It was first fitted to a CB600F Hornet in 2003. HISS features a small electronic device inside the starter key known as a transponder. The ignition system will only switch on to start the engine if it detects the transponder in the key. Without it, the bike is immobilised, making it harder to steal.

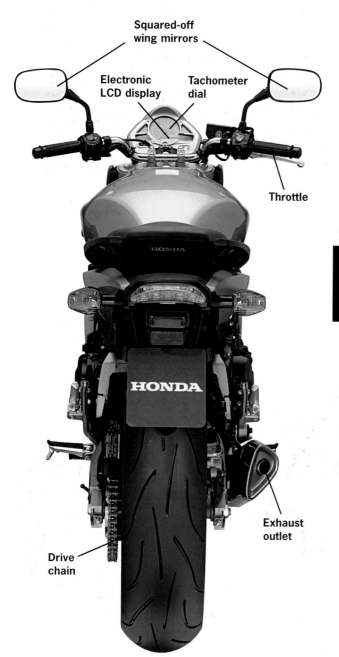

Squared-off wing mirrors

Electronic LCD display

Tachometer dial

Throttle

Drive chain

Exhaust outlet

⬆ The Hornet's optional tankbag attaches to the fuel tank with magnets. It has a 13-litre capacity and also contains a see-through map pocket and a built-in rain cover.

Tech talk

Immobilised – when a bike is prevented from starting.

Tachometer – a device that measures the revolutions (revs) of a motorbike engine and displays them to the rider.

Transponder – a wireless device which responds to a radio signal.

Honda CR85R

Motocross is an affordable motorsport that has more riders than any other form of motorbike racing. The Honda CR85R is an entry level machine for beginner and intermediate riders, but is packed with advanced features. It is used for motocross racing and general off-road riding over tough terrain.

⬆ A motocross rider puts a CR85R through its paces, ploughing through a muddy turn, keeping the bike moving and his body balanced.

Full throttle facts

Top speed: 96 kph
Length: 1,803 mm

Ground clearance: 311 mm
Fuel capacity: 5.3 litres

Engine and drive train guard

Fold-up foot peg

⬆ *Foot pegs fold up when they are not needed and are cleated to offer excellent grip. A rider stands on them to lift up off the seat over large bumps.*

The bike wheel size

The CR85R comes in two versions with different wheel sizes. The CR85R has a 14-inch back wheel and 17-inch front wheel. The CR85R2 features larger wheels (19-inch front and 16-inch rear).

Rider position

Off-road riding requires excellent balance. The CR85R has a long, slim, banana-shaped seat with a non-slip surface. This seat allows riders to move their bodyweight forward or backward from the handlebars. They do this to keep the bike under control up and down steep hills and drops.

Tech talk

Cleated – fitted with studs to help grip.

Motocross – off-road race of around 40 riders over rough ground and jumps.

Kerb weight: 75 kg
Seat height: 824 mm

Engine capacity: 85 cc
Gearbox: 6-speed

Tough terrain

Motocross is an incredibly popular and exciting motorsport. Up to 40 riders start a race over a number of laps on an off-road circuit. The circuit contains challenges in the terrain including hills, ditches and jumps. High-quality motocross bikes, such as the CR85R, have to be light, tough and able to accelerate quickly at low speeds. They need only a small fuel tank, but must have hard, chunky tyres with a deep tread pattern to grip the soft ground.

Ground clearance

Off-road and motocross riding often involves travelling over large bumps and obstacles, such as logs and boulders.

The CR85R has a high ground clearance of 311 mm so that it can be ridden up and over obstacles without damaging the bike.

HOT SPOT

Shock absorbers

Shock absorbers are air or oil-filled cylinders connected to the wheel axles. The CR85R features very large shock absorbers that can travel, or move up and down, a long way. These cushion some of the impact from heavy landings in motocross riding. The CR85R's front shock absorber can travel up to 245 mm, and the rear up to 275 mm.

⊖ The CR85R has very simple controls that are all within easy reach so riders can concentrate on their path ahead. The levers

Honda CR85R

Wide rear mudguard

Banana-shaped seat

Kickstart lever to start bike

Front mudguard

Long travel suspension

Aluminium rim wheels

Lightweight liquid-cooled 85 cc engine

High ground clearance

Chunky-tread tyres for maximum grip

Rear 190 mm diameter disc brake

Front 220 mm diameter disc brake

⬆ *A rider lifts up from the seat of his CR85R as he races off-road. He is wearing a motocross helmet, goggles, gloves, boots and leathers.*

Honda Shadow VT750C

Honda began selling the Shadow range of motorbikes in 1983. These cruiser-type machines have an upright riding style and widely spaced handlebars, making the bikes comfortable to ride over long distances. The latest Shadow, the VT750C, has lots of chrome detailing, a long wheelbase and a V-twin engine.

↑ A rider cruises down a dirt road onboard a brand new Honda Shadow 750. The rider sits upright with his feet positioned ahead of the body for a clear view of the road ahead.

Full throttle facts

Top speed: 160 kph
Length: 2,505 mm

Ground clearance: 130.8 mm
Fuel capacity: 14 litres

Tech talk

Cylinders – the parts of the engine where fuel and air are ignited to produce power.

Detailing – when a small part of something is given special treatment.

Wheelbase – the distance from the rear axle to the front axle.

HOT SPOT

Engine configurations

Engine configuration usually means the number of cylinders an engine has and the pattern they are laid out in. The CBR1000RR Fireblade (see pages 26–29) has an inline 4 configuration, with four cylinders placed all in a straight row.

The Honda Shadow has a V-twin configuration. This means that the engine's two cylinders are placed at a V-shaped angle. In the Shadow VT750C's case the cylinders are angled 52 degrees apart.

⬆ *The Shadow VT750C's V-shaped engine is clearly visible in this photograph.*

Kerb weight: 254.3 kg
Seat height: 658 mm

Engine capacity: 745 cc
Gearbox: 5-speed

The Shadow series

The Shadow series was introduced as a replacement for the older Honda Rebel. It was aimed particularly at the American bike market, where cruiser-type bikes are very popular. The first Shadow bikes were the VT500C and VT750C models. Over the years, the Shadow series has included small 125 cc models, as well as the 2004 Shadow Sabre, which boasted a large 1099 cc liquid-cooled engine.

In 2006, the model range reduced to just the Shadow VT750C – although the Shadow Spirit appeared in 2007. The VT750C can carry a load of up to 180 kg. This equals an adult rider and passenger, plus a full load in the saddlebags with weight to spare.

Luggage options

The Shadow VT750C luggage options:
- leather saddlebags
- a backrest bag
- a leather handlebar pouch
- a rear carrier
- a magnetic tankbag.

Tech talk

Clutch – the device that lets the rider select a gear.

Speedometer – displays the speed at which the bike is travelling.

Tripometer – a display of the distance travelled which can be reset to zero by the rider.

← *The Honda Shadow VT750C has an unusually large speedometer mounted on top of the bike's 14 litre fuel tank. It includes a tripometer.*

Round, classic-style rear-view side mirrors

Clutch lever

Front indicator lamp

18-litre capacity leather saddlebag set fitted over the rear of the bike

Gear selector

Front fork

Transmission

Many smaller motorbikes transmit their power from the engine to their rear wheel using a drive chain. The Shadow VT750C uses a drive shaft rather than a chain to power the rear wheel. The rider selects the bike's five gears using a foot-operated lever whilst using the clutch with his or her hand.

Shadow VT750C

Flat seat for pillion passenger

Electric starter on handlebars

Large front disc brake

Wheelbase measures 1,639 mm

V-twin 745 cc engine

Steel rimmed, wire-spoked wheels

Honda Gold Wing GL1800

The Honda Gold Wing is one of the most famous motorbike models in the world. Thousands of riders and their passengers have enjoyed cruising over long distances on these powerful machines. The latest Goldwing model, the GL1800, is the ultimate in motorbike luxury. It has a powerful 80-watt sound system with six speakers, and a push-button electric reverse gear.

⬆ *The Honda Goldwing GL1800 is big enough for two people to travel comfortably over long distances.*

Comfort package

The Gold Wing GL1800 comes with a comfort package for cold weather cruising. This includes electric handlebar grip heaters and a seat heater system for both the rider and passenger. Both functions are adjustable to six different temperature settings.

⬅ *This close-up of the GL1800's central console shows the ignition key and one of the seat heater setting dials.*

Full throttle facts

Top speed: 210 kph +
Length: 2,635 mm

Ground clearance: 125 mm
Fuel capacity: 25 litres

HOT SPOT

Satellite navigation

The GL1800 comes with satellite navigation (sat nav). This system receives signals from satellites orbiting the Earth to help people work out their precise position when travelling around.

The Gold Wing's sat nav system is programmed with locations of Honda dealers and petrol stations, and can be controlled using the rider's voice.

⊘ The Gold Wing GL1800's high-tech control panel includes an intercom system which lets the rider and passenger speak to each other clearly.

Kerb weight: 405 kg
Seat height: 740 mm

Engine capacity: 1832 cc
Gearbox: 5-speed

Golden history

In 2005, the Gold Wing celebrated its 30th anniversary. The very first Gold Wing featured a 999 cc, 4-cylinder engine. In 1980 the first GL1100 model was sold, with a lockable boot and a large fairing. In 1988, the bike grew in size again. The engine became a 6-cylinder, 1520 cc beast and a reverse gear was added because of the machine's large size. The first GL1800 bike arrived in 2001. The 2006 version, fully loaded and fuelled, can weigh around 602 kg, almost the same as a Formula One racing car.

Gold Wing GL1800 colour options

- Black-Z
- Billet Silver Metallic
- Cabernet Red Metallic

Honda Gold Wing GL1800

Front speakers

Rear speakers

Rear boot

Shaped passenger seat

Clear windshield

Large panniers

Stainless steel exhaust system

6-cylinder 1832 cc engine

Front 5-spoke wheel made of hollow cast aluminium

Motorbike airbag

The Gold Wing GL1800 is one of Honda's first bikes to be fitted with an airbag system to help protect the rider should there be a crash. Four sensors mounted on the front fork of the motorbike send information about speed to the ECU (engine control unit). The ECU decides if a very sharp change in speed is a crash or just hard braking. If it thinks it is a crash, it triggers the airbag. This inflates with gas to help protect the rider from a front impact.

Twin-beam dual headlights

Front double disc brake

Tech talk

ECU – short for engine control unit which is a computer that controls many of the engine's functions.

Formula One – the top class of specialised motorcar racing on a circuit.

Inflates – to be blown up with gas, like a balloon.

Panniers – storage bins or boxes made to fit on the sides of a bike.

Sensors – devices that measure something around them, such as speed or temperature.

Honda PS125i

Honda motorbikes first produced motor scooters with small engines for the Japanese market. Today, scooters are a popular alternative to cars for commuters all over the world. They cost far less to buy and maintain. The PS125i motor scooter was introduced in 2006. It has a steel frame with a fuel-injected, liquid-cooled 125 cc engine. Its sister model, the PS150i, has a slightly larger engine.

⬆ One option for the PS125i is a rugged windshield made of a tough plastic called polycarbonate. The windscreen includes knuckle visors to shield the rider's hands.

⬆ The PS125i's 125 cc engine provides enough power to allow two people to ride comfortably on the scooter's long seat.

Full throttle facts

Top speed: 80 kph
Length: 1,990 mm

Ground clearance: 125 mm
Fuel capacity: 8 litres

Engine and emissions

The PS125i's 4-stroke engine is very economical, which means it uses less fuel over a longer distance. The scooter is also one of the cleanest bikes around. It uses an advanced control system and produces very low emissions from its exhaust.

Colour options
• Max Grey Metallic (with Fury Red)
• Interstellar Black Metallic (with Ardesia Grey)
• Winter Lake Blue Metallic (with Ardesia Grey)
• Candy Xenon Blue (with Ardesia Grey)

↑ The PS125i's liquid-cooled engine is tucked away under the bike's seat.

Tech talk

Emissions – the harmful gases released from a motor vehicle's exhaust into the atmosphere.

Fuel injection – a system that carefully controls the amount of fuel entering an engine cylinder.

Motor scooter – a small motorbike with a step-through frame, usually with an engine size of between 50 cc and 400 cc.

Kerb weight: 126 kg
Seat height: 800 mm

Engine capacity: 125 cc
Gearbox: automatic

Riding position

The PS125i has been carefully designed to give a comfortable, upright riding position. It has a higher driving position than many scooters, with the seat 800 mm from the ground. This gives the rider a good view of the road and traffic. It has a large, flat footboard, allowing riders to place their feet in many different positions. The side bodywork narrows in the middle of the scooter to allow the feet to reach the floor easily.

55–60-watt front headlight

Brake levers

Front indicator lamps

Air inlets to cool radiator

Honda PS125i

Brake light

Rear wheel mudguard

Seat height 800 mm from ground

Throttle

Fold-up bike stand

Footboard

6-spoke wheels made from cast aluminium

Brakes

The PS125i features a combined brake system. The right-side brake lever controls the front brake, a 220 mm disc brake. The left lever operates both the front brake and the 130 mm rear drum brake. This makes it easier for beginner riders to control the scooter while keeping a grip on the throttle.

Cool down

The PS125i's engine radiator is built into the scooter's nose. The air inlets (left) are positioned directly below the headlight, between the front indicator lamps. They help the radiator to receive a blast of air when powering forward. The radiator keeps the engine cool and running at its ideal temperature.

Tech talk

Disc brake – a brake system where brake pads press onto a disc attached to the motorbike wheel. This action slows the bike down and stops the wheel from turning.

Drum brake – a brake system where a set of brake pads press against a cylinder attached to the motorbike wheel. It works in the same way as a disk brake.

Radiator – a water-filled cooling system that reduces the temperature of the engine and stops it overheating. Fan-assisted radiators are also blasted by an electric fan.

Honda CBR1000RR Fireblade

Back in 1992, Honda released their first Fireblade motorbike; the CBR900RR. It was designed by Mr Tadao Baba. It aimed to have the power and raw speed of a larger bike, equipped with a 900 cc engine, but turn and handle like a smaller, 600 cc machine.

At the time the Fireblade revolutionised fast, powerful supersport bikes. It was a lot lighter and more agile than any of its rivals. The latest Fireblade model, the CBR1000RR, continues the trend.

⬆ Sleek lines, very high power and low weight add up to make the CBR1000RR Fireblade a top performer both on the road and in track-based racing competitions.

Full throttle facts

Top speed: 260 kph +
Length: 2,030 mm

Ground clearance: 130 mm
Fuel capacity: 18 litres

Red hot racer

The 2006 Fireblade's engine is tuned to perform well at high speeds. Its maximum torque level is 10,000 rpm, whereas the previous model peaked at 8,500 rpm. The motorbike can accelerate from a standing start to 100 km/h in less than three seconds.

➜ The Fireblade's instrument panel features a digital speedometer and a large tachometer dial with its redline starting at 12,500 rpm.

Tech talk

Redline – maximum safe engine speed for a motorbike. It is often shown on a tachometer dial in red.

Rpm – short for revolutions per minute; a measurement of the speed of a motorbike's engine.

Torque – the force produced by an engine to move the drive chain which powers the rear wheel of the motorbike.

⬆ This protective cover is specially made to fit the Honda Fireblade.

Kerb weight: 203 kg
Seat height: 831 mm

Engine capacity: 998 cc
Gearbox: 6-speed

Input from racing

From 2004 onwards, the Fireblade models were designed and built using input from Honda's successful MotoGP racing team. Their experience and technology helped to produce better bikes. The latest Fireblade features a lightweight aluminium frame and a weight-forward design. This means the bike can get more power to the ground quicker when coming out of corners.

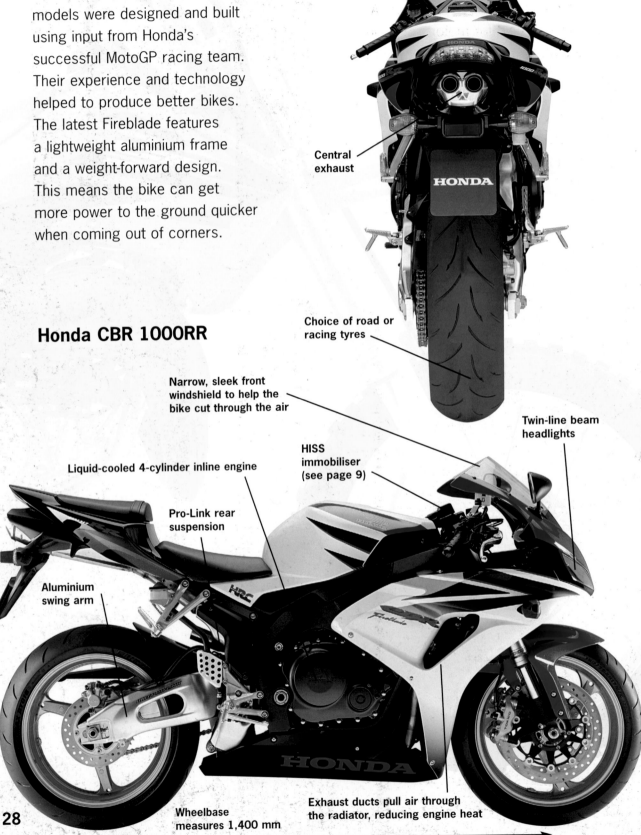

Central exhaust

Choice of road or racing tyres

Honda CBR 1000RR

Narrow, sleek front windshield to help the bike cut through the air

Twin-line beam headlights

HISS immobiliser (see page 9)

Liquid-cooled 4-cylinder inline engine

Pro-Link rear suspension

Aluminium swing arm

Wheelbase measures 1,400 mm

Exhaust ducts pull air through the radiator, reducing engine heat

Le Mans Moto

The Le Mans 24 Hours is one of the most famous car races in the world. A version is also held for motorbikes, the 24 Hours Moto. It is an awesome test of both the riders and their bikes' speed, stamina and reliability. The 2006 race was won by a Honda Fireblade, which notched up more than 800 laps in the 24 hours of continuous racing.

Tech talk

MotoGP – a top competition in motorbike circuit racing.

Swing arm – the movable joint between the motorbike frame and the rear axle. It supports the rear wheel and its suspension parts.

The No.55 Honda Fireblade, ridden over 24 hours by a team of three riders: Dani Ribalta, Olivier Four and Frédéric Protat, on its way to winning the 2006 Le Mans 24 Hours Moto, two laps ahead of its nearest rival.

Glossary

Axle – the central shaft that a wheel spins round.

cc – short for cubic centimetres, this is used as a measurement of the size of the engine's cylinders.

Cruiser – a motorbike usually with a small petrol tank, an upright riding style and feet-forward seating.

Drive chain – similar to a bicycle chain, this is a chain that transmits power from the engine to the rear wheel.

Foot pegs – rests or short poles that stick out from the sides of the bike and give riders somewhere to place their feet.

Grip – the ability of a vehicle to stay connected to the ground. Also refers to the ends of the handlebars that the rider holds.

Handling – the way a motorbike responds when being ridden, such as how it turns into and out of corners.

Horsepower (hp) – a unit of measurement used for giving the amount of power an engine generates.

Kickstart lever – a foot pedal used to start the engine of some motorbikes. Other motorbikes have an electric starter.

kph – kilometres per hour; a measurement of speed.

Pillion – the backseat on a motorbike for its passenger.

Saddlebags – containers that hang over the sides of the bike behind the rider.

Shock absorbers – devices that are designed to absorb sudden forces and impacts to the suspension of the vehicle.

Suspension – the system of springs, shock absorbers and other components, directly connected to the wheels or the axles to help create a smooth ride. Changes to suspension levels affect the handling of a race vehicle.

Swing arm – a movable joint between the frame of the motorbike and the rear axle.

Tachometer – a dial or display that tells the rider the speed of the engine in revolutions per minute (rpm).

Throttle – a device that controls the flow of fuel to an engine – the faster the flow, the higher the speed.

Wheelbase – the distance between the front and rear axles of a vehicle.

Further information

Websites

http://www.honda-eu.com
The official website of Honda in Europe. This website is full of pictures and details of Honda's latest bikes.

http://motorcycles.about.com/od/hondaother
A handy list of links to other Honda websites, produced by the About.com network.

http://www.hoc.org.uk/gallery/index.html
A great picture gallery of Honda motorbikes brought to you by the Honda Owners Club of Great Britain.

http://www.bikez.com/brand/honda_motorcycles.php
An enormous list of major Honda motorbike models from the 1970s to the present day. Click on a link to learn more about each bike including its specifications.

Books

The Honda Story
Ian Falloon (Haynes Group, 2005).
An in-depth guide to Honda's road and racing motorbikes from the 1940s to the present day.

Honda Production Motorcycles 1946–1980
Mick Walker (Crowood Press, 2006).
Featuring Honda motorcycles from the classic era, including the Gold Wing.

Honda Motorcycles: The Ultimate Guide
Doug Mitchel (Krause Publications, 2005).
A photo-packed look at Honda's motorbikes through the decades.

Motorcycle Touring Bible
Fred Rau (Motorbooks International, 2010).
Find about all about motorcycle touring and the equipment you would need. Includes photographs.

Honda timeline

1948 – Honda Motor Co. Ltd is founded in Japan.

1949 – Honda's first motorbike, the 98 cc Dream D, is produced.

1959 – Honda makes its first appearance in motorbike racing at the Isle of Man TT.

1963 – Honda opens its first overseas factory in Belgium.

1973 – Company founder, Mr Soichiro Honda, retires.

1974 – The first Honda Gold Wing, the GL1000, is put on sale in the United States of America.

1976 – Honda produces its first motorbike with automatic gears, the CB750A Hondamatic.

1983 – Honda introduces its first version of the Shadow.

1992 – Honda produce their first Fireblade, the CBR900RR.

1998 – The first Honda CB600 Hornet is produced, sparking interest in naked bikes.

2005 – Honda produces its 150 millionth motorbike. Honda records its 600th win in World championship Grand Prix racing, more than any other manufacturer.

2006 – An exciting new supersports bike, CBR1000RR FireBlade, is released.

2012 – A limited edition of the new 690 Duke is launched.

Index